I've Always Paddled My Own Canoe

I've Always Paddled My Own Canoe

MEURIG JONES — Resident of Loose Kent

StoryTerrace

The key to happiness is to have dreams.
The key to success is to make dreams come true.

CONTENTS

1. I'VE ALWAYS PADDLED MY OWN CANOE   9

2. EUROPE   15

3. ASIA AND MALAYSIA   29

4. AUSTRALIA   81

5. THE WAY BACK   97

6. JUST A LAD FROM LLANDINAM   115

MY JOURNEY   117

1. I'VE ALWAYS PADDLED MY OWN CANOE

From the age of about 10, all I wanted to do was leave the small Welsh village of Llandinam where I was born. I would hitch-hike wherever I could go, sometimes to Liverpool for the day. At 16, I hitch-hiked to Paris and slept under the Eiffel Tower and on the embankment with the meths drinkers. I always knew my horizons stretched beyond the fields, beyond that farm, beyond my wagoner father's footsteps. The youngest and most adventurous of three brothers, I would dream of those faraway countries whose stamps I collected and whose borders I could draw from memory and I'd long to go there. And then, in 1971, my dreams came true.

Llandinam is a small farming village in Montgomeryshire in central Wales. Everyone knows everyone else and if any of us three boys stepped out of line, the policeman who lived next door would tell our dad. A hard-working wagoner and a stern, distant father, Dad got paid once a year and we'd only see him on a Sunday morning when he came home to the seven-acre smallholding that Mum worked to keep our household going. He wanted a better future for his three sons – his vision for us just didn't include my travelling the world.

My parents never travelled. The only breaks Dad ever had from work were in the autumn when he had to take the shire horses to the shows in Shrewsbury or Oswestry. Mum would take us to my uncle, aunts and cousins for the holidays and, apart from enjoying a change of scenery, I enjoyed watching Uncle Richie smoke a pipe that he'd fashioned out of a cotton reel. I learnt to smoke on those holidays and, when I got my first job unloading lorries, I used my wages to buy cigarettes.

When I was 11, Mum got me a job at Penstrowed Garage. Everyone in the area came to the garage for petrol and I got to talk to them all; my conversations with policemen, mayors, school teachers, the director of education, newspaper reporters and the like awakened in me a longing to experience the world outside of Llandinam. I worked at the garage part-time for the next 17 years – through school, teachers' training college and my early years of working as a teacher.

I was always good with my hands, and my woodwork teacher inspired me to become a teacher. In sixth form, I opted to do woodwork instead of Latin and also became the first pupil at my school to do A-Level technical drawing and metalwork. After school, I went to teachers' training college in Bristol and then got my first job as a teacher at a school there.

I never lost my longing to travel and, in 1968, when I suggested to some of the sixth formers at my school that after school and before uni we should go on a trip to Athens, they agreed. I got to work planning my first proper long trip and nine of us set off from Bristol in my Thames Ford 15 van with a three-speed engine, otherwise known as the Dagenham Dustbin. We arrived in Athens eight days later and were away for about six weeks. One evening, while we were sitting on the beach in the small fishing village of Dafni in Zakynthos, a vehicle arrived that would inspire and foretell my life-changing, intercontinental road trip.

The words 'Paris to Nepal' on the side of the vehicle got us intrigued. I don't know if it was the beer talking or just teenage enthusiasm, but all nine of us agreed that on my dad's birthday in three years' time, 1st September 1971, we'd all leave Bristol and travel by road to Australia. I'd made an Australian friend who'd been in Bristol on a teaching exchange and it seemed like a good and distant destination to aim for.

When we got back home, I bought a split-screen VW van and started working on it and, as I'd feared, the teenage enthusiasm wore off. Over the next few years, all of the original nine dropped out. I wasn't really surprised as many of them were studying, starting out in their careers and in new relationships. But I kept working on the van, still determined to go.

I put an ad in The Guardian newspaper, and I had about 70 replies from all around the world. I chatted to a lot of the applicants and found my first two co-travellers: Sandra from Kingston upon Thames and Don from Brigg in Lincolnshire. The three of us continued to interview other applicants but, in the end, we decided it would be just the three of us who would go. I resigned from my teaching post, although the headmaster kept my job open as he didn't think I'd go, and then all I needed to do was tell my parents.

I always knew my mum and dad wouldn't be happy. The first time I applied for a passport, I knew my dad would never sign the application form so I forged his signature and travelled to the next town to apply, as I wouldn't get away with that in a village where everyone knew us. So when I told my family I was going away on a long overland trip and I wouldn't be home for Christmas and Easter, my dad walked out. Mum wasn't happy, but she at least gave me her blessing – she knew she couldn't stop me from going.

On the last Saturday in August 1971, I went to the garage to say goodbye to the people who worked there, and the owners asked if I could look after the garage for the day while they went out. A guy came in while I was polishing my van, and he happened to work for the local newspaper. 'You're joking,' he said, when I told him what I was doing and where my van would be taking me over the coming months. He asked if he could take a photo, so I got the guys who worked in the garage, who'd helped me with the van, to stand next to the van too. The journalist took a picture and wrote an article, which appeared on the front page of The Montgomeryshire County Times the Saturday after I left. The headline read: 'Off on seven-month journey.'

Sunday was my day to say goodbye to my parents. They were at a festival in the chapel at Newchapel and I went there to see them. I was dreading it; it wasn't an easy thing for me to do but I knew they wouldn't be happy at all. I was right. When I said goodbye to Dad, he walked away without saying goodbye to me. Mum said, 'Just look after yourself,' and I promised I would.

I'd always been the son with the biggest dreams. The one who had moved away, who had long dreamt of seeing the world and who was determined not to follow the path laid out for a boy who grew up in a small village in the heart of Wales.

Wide, endless horizons now lay before me. I'd envisaged a journey that would take me across the world and I never gave up hope that it would happen, just as I'd said on that Greek beach three years before. On my dad's birthday, Wednesday 1st September 1971, the three of us left London for Australia in a camper van.

I've always paddled my own canoe.

Off on seven-month journey

Christmas for school teacher, Meurig Jones, of Llandinam, will be a little different this year. For he hopes to celebrate it at Katmandu, on the south side of Mount Everest.

With two friends, he set out this week on a seven-month journey which will take him 10,000 miles across land to Australia.

Each mile he covers will have a special meaning for the pupils of the Bristol school where he is head of the metal work department.

For each mile travelled the children will sponsor their teacher, donating the money to o.

local charities. "We shall be making a bee-line for Istanbul, said Meurig, who is the son of Mr. and Mrs. R. M. Jones, Green Lane, Llandinam.

"We hope to just get over the Khyber Pass before the snow." For transport they have a £300 Volkswagen Dormobile which has been put through its paces at Penstrowed Garage, where Meurig works during the holidays. The whole venture is expected to cost the three friends £448 each.

After a ferry trip from Dover to Ostend, they will motor through Belgium, Germany, Austria, Yugoslavia, Greece and Turkey. "Our biggest worry is the vehicle. If that goes well we won't have many problems,"

Mechanics Alan Rodgers, Eddie Jones, and Alan Joseph give Meurig Jones a send-off on Monday, when he left to travel over-land to Australia.

he told a County Times and Express reporter.

Just in case they have any breakdowns, they will take along a spare gearbox,four spare tyres, plus Meurig's expert knowledge. In all he estimates the Volkswagen will drink 400 gallons of petrol on the journey.

In Malaya and Nepal they intend to stop to make short visits, before boarding the ferry to Freemantle, Perth, on April

5. In Australia the three will work for five months to raise money for the return trip.

"Most of our money will go on ferries," said Meurig as he did some last minute adjustments on the vehicle. Any problems they encounter on their marathon holiday should be quickly ironed out. One of his companions is a legal adviser from Brigg, Lincolnshire, and the third is a social worker from London.

Mongomeryshire County Times, 3rd Sept 1971

2. EUROPE

After picking up Don and Sandra, we went into London to buy some tea chests and basic food and other supplies, and then made our way down to Dover to catch the ferry to Calais. It was quite exciting to think that, after close on three years of planning and working on the van, we were leaving on this epic adventure.

As I'd put together the whole journey for the original group, Don and Sandra were happy to fall in with those arrangements. I had a good idea of what I wanted our route to be, and we stuck pretty much to it, with the flexibility, of course, to be spontaneous and to visit other places that people told us about along the way. And we did plenty of that.

I'd also worked out a budget for the trip; each of us needed to contribute the princely sum of £445 towards the central budget. We put part of that into a bank account, for our ferry trip to Australia and for any other big expenses. The rest of the cash we put into blocks, along with our own money, and we hid it in three different places in the van to keep it safe.

Before we set off we discussed whether or not to write our destination on the side of the van, like those 'Paris to Nepal' words that had inspired the trip originally. We didn't do that, as I felt if people knew where we were going, they'd know we had money and goods, and that would put us at risk. We also talked about whether or not to take a gun with us. I'm pleased to say we decided against it, as it would have been one extra thing to worry about, plus it could just as easily have been used against us. Most of the time we were very sensible and, as it happened, we never needed a gun anyway.

Don and I shared the driving but I did most of it, mainly because it was my van and I'd been working on it for the past three years to get it ready for the long journey. We carried a spare gearbox on the roof, along with a good supply of petrol, which we kept replenishing en route.

It was also no small matter that we didn't really know each other. We'd only met when Don and Sandra responded to my ad in The Guardian, and now we were all going to be living together in a very confined space, making lifelong memories and taking on a journey of a lifetime together. How was it all going to work? I thought some ground rules would be helpful, so I told Don and Sandra that I felt we needed to be honest with each other all the time, and always say what annoyed us about anyone's behaviour or habits or anything else, before anything got out of hand – as they often do. The only thing that came up straight away was that Sandra was fussy about how people squeezed toothpaste out of a tube. So whatever it was she didn't like, Don and I didn't ever do!

Setting those basic ground rules seemed to work well; we were together for eight months, living together like a small family, and we didn't fall out at all. When it came to chores, we seemed to share them out quite naturally too – there were never any issues about who should do what, and it never felt like any one of us was not pulling our weight. Don was good at buying meat; both he and Sandra were better than me at shopping and cooking; and I was happy to drive and look after the vehicle and keep some kind of order in it.

Our meals were simple and we tended to have two a day: breakfast, which was cornflakes and milk, sometimes eggs on toast (with no butter), or fruit; and a main meal that was usually meat and two veg. The van had a gas cooker so we carried gas bottles with us and refilled them where and when we could. A funny food story is that when we got to Australia, the authorities confiscated a tin of peaches that we'd bought in London and carried all the way with us. What's even funnier is that the peaches came from South Australia! Money was tight and so was space, so we lived as simply and frugally as possible. We never stayed in campsites, we parked wherever we could, and we all slept in the van – it had a raised roof, so two people could sleep at the top, or on the flattened seats. We carried our own water and sometimes washed ourselves in the sea, otherwise we'd find somewhere local, for example a hammam (Turkish bath) in Istanbul, where you could shower and have a massage (a guy walked on your back). We'd use the toilets at garages when we filled up with petrol; some of those toilets were terrible, in fact most of them weren't too special, but we managed OK. And then, at my instigation, we stopped on the last day of every month to clean and repack everything in the van. It was a good discipline.

Another good discipline for me was writing regularly to the school and to the newspaper, The Montgomeryshire County Times, to keep them informed of my progress. I'd write from key stops along the way, which I knew the pupils at Monks Park School would be following closely. My class had made a huge map of the world, which they put up in the foyer of the school so they could map the progress of my trip. The school had also decided to use it as a vehicle for raising funds for their chosen charity – I can't remember which one it was, but the pupils would get 'sponsored' for each leg of the trip I'd completed. When my letters arrived at the school, they would pin each one to the relevant spot on the map, along with photographs and key facts that I'd included about each place. I wanted to make it interesting and, at the same time, for the children to learn about the places I was visiting. But the school soon had to take the map down as there were too many children gathering around it to read the letters, and this was causing congestion in the foyer! The school's typing teacher then took it upon herself to type out every one of my letters as they arrived, make copies of them on the Banda machine, and then give a copy to each class. I've kept all of those letters I wrote, although some of them never made it out of the post offices I sent them from. For example, I discovered that in Kabul, they steamed the stamps off my letters and threw the letters away, so those ones never arrived.

Back to the road trip. Our first stop was going to be Istanbul in Turkey, and we stopped over in Greece along the way. I remember one night where the night sky was crystal clear, with the full moon gleaming onto the crisp, clear earth; it was absolutely glorious. After six days and having driven our first 1,800 miles, we reached Istanbul. We drove straight to the Blue Mosque and parked our van outside it. I don't think you could do anything like that today, but that was where we slept for the next few nights. There was a place nearby where you could wash your feet, so we washed our clothes in there too. And every morning we were woken up with a knock on our van door, and a little boy standing there offering us 'Chai, chai, sweetmeats, chai!' It was a good trade for him, and a lovely little ritual for us.

After washing, we'd plan our day, which sometimes including going for a haircut, writing letters, or going to the post office to collect or send mail. You may wonder how I had mail to collect, but my friends and family (and the school) knew which dates I was likely to be somewhere, so they'd address my letters to that particular place, poste restante. This meant it would go to the town or city's main post office and it would remain there a certain amount of time, for collection by the addressee. It was such a valuable service, as it kept us travellers in contact with our friends and families back home.

Our evenings in Istanbul were quite magical, especially when we went down to the Galata Bridge at sunset. That's when and where the fishing boats would come in. So we'd get there in time to greet the fishing boats, and then the fishermen would barbecue the fish, put some of it between two pieces of bread and sell it to us. That was our dinner and it was absolutely delicious.

We also enjoyed going to the Grand Bazaar, which dates back to the mid-1400s and is one of the biggest and oldest covered markets in the world. It covers an enormous amount of ground, includes 61 covered streets and has about 2,000 arches. You could buy anything there from a pin to a fridge to an air-conditioning unit. We couldn't buy anything, of course, as we had no room or money for anything extra, but we enjoyed watching the Armenian porters, known as hamals, carry heavy goods home for buyers. They'd walk with the incredibly heavy and cumbersome goods on their backs, with their heads to the ground, and they'd shout at everyone to move out of their path.

There were so many other places to visit in Istanbul. We went up the Bosphorous, to the edge of the Black Sea, and to Topkapi Palace, the administrative centre and main residence of the sultans of the Ottoman Empire from the mid-1400s to the mid-1800s. I couldn't believe how much gold there was there, it was breathtaking. We also went to the St Sophia Mosque, got a boat to Troy and on to Ephesus, and made our way around the coast, before heading inland to Pamukkale. This is an outdoor amphitheatre in an outcrop of calcium (it's known as 'the iced cake') and, as the sun sets, the glow turns the white rocks into a colourful, red spectacle, which is absolutely exquisite. We stayed there and treated ourselves to a beer and, by this stage, Don was starting to look like a local!

We then went round the south and parked in a wood that overlooked the sea. We needed to work on a few things on the van: underneath and on top of the engine, and an oil change. Don had been a sidecar rider for the Isle of Man TT, so he knew about mechanics and everything but, as I'd rebuilt the engine with the students at school, I knew that I knew more about the car than he did! Don worked on the top of the engine and I did the rest. I was convinced Don had put the plug leads back on in the wrong firing order, but he was adamant he hadn't. In that sort of situation, I tend to give people the benefit of the doubt but I really had a nagging suspicion I was right . . .

Once we'd finished all of that, we travelled to Antalya on the south coast, after driving through beautiful rocky formations running along the edge of a narrow plain. The coast road from Antalya towards Adana crossed several ridges and the journey was a constant pass for 30km. At Silifki, we turned north towards Konya.

Life on the road was interesting, and our best times were meeting new friends and fellow travellers along the way. But some friends weren't ones we'd wanted to make, like the time we discovered we weren't travelling alone. Before we left Antalya, we'd heard a scratching noise in the van at night and, when we noticed something had also been nibbling away at our stuff, we realised we had a stowaway – a mouse! We kept hoping we could catch it but it kept outsmarting us.

Konya, which appeared in the heart of Turkey like a green patch on a brown piece of paper. It was here that we saw the dances of the whirling dervishes, who practise a fascinating and ancient worshipful ritual that is part dance, prayer, meditation and trance.

We continued onto Ankara and, by the time we got there, the van's engine was really struggling. We found a VW garage and they told us both cylinder heads had cracked and we'd also burnt out two valves. Not a great way to end the first leg of our journey.

Our next leg would take us to Iran.

Blue Mosque, Istanbul

Chay (Turkish Tea)

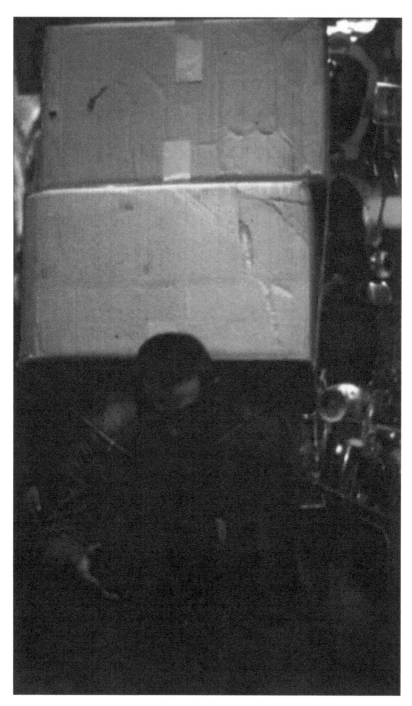

Armenian Porter in the Grand Bazaar.

Pamukkale (Hot springs in South Turkey)

Lunar landscape in the Goreme Valley

The roads having an effect on our tyres

3. ASIA AND MALAYSIA

We arrived at the borders of Turkey and Iran at Bazargan. Here, we had our clocks moved forward ninety minutes, which meant we were now two-and-a-half hours ahead of England. After having everything checked, we left on a beautiful highway towards Tabrig and each night we were in Iran, we arrived either at the highway petrol centres or the central police station. In fact, they were very helpful. Some even gave us fruit and vegetables from their garden.

When we arrived in Tabrig, we changed our minds about travelling south to Kermsha, and decided instead to drive to Tehran, then south to Qom, Isfahan and Shiraz, and return on the same route.

Isfahan is situated on a high plateau and is said to be "half the world". It lies on the River Zeyandeh in the centre of a fertile plain. Its history goes back to the 6th century B.C.. Maidin-e Shah is the main Square, said to be one of the largest in the world. Two Mosques, a Palace and the Bazaar, all face the centre of the square.

There, we saw the amazing Shah Mosque, known for being the most important example of Persian architecture in the Islamic era. We also visited the Ali Qapu Palace, which is now a World Heritage Site. From there, we drove up to Tehran, where we stayed for four days before moving on to Qom, one of Iran's religious cities.

On our first evening in Qom, we went into a transport cafe for supper and, as you'd expect, it was a rough and ready establishment, with sawdust on the floor. When we saw the place was crawling with cockroaches too, we probably should have opted out, but we didn't. We stayed and had a delicious lamb curry. After our meal, we drove out of the city to park outside the army barracks. We'd been told if we did that, the sentry could keep an eye on our vehicle. But what happened was, our delicious lamb curry must have come with a side order of the runs, which wasn't fun at all. After a night of us all dashing out of the van in different directions, we felt we needed a couple of days to recover, so we stayed where we were.

Once that had passed, as it were, we left Qom for Persepolis and then travelled onto Shiraz on the Persian Gulf. We'd noticed that the van was losing oil, so once we got to Shiraz we took the engine out, stripped it and rebuilt it. We spent a couple of days doing this, working on a drum in the middle of nowhere, much to the amazement of all the lorry drivers that used to come in every morning and evening. Don had, in fact, put the valves back in the wrong firing order, but far be it for me to say I told you so . . .

We then drove from Shiraz back up to Tehran. The roads from the south cross vast plains edged by the low mountains. The road rolls out like an everlasting steel rule, and you may travel ten miles without a bend. We were pleased to arrive in Tehran, even though it was only to collect the mail we were expecting.

The barrier of the Elburz, between Tehran and the Caspian, is negotiated by the most dramatic highways in Iran. There is a long climb to the pass, past the Spa of Abali, then a new winter sports centre, and near to the circuitous route to the Valley of the Assassins, inaccessible six months of the year. It comes almost to the base of Mount Damavand (at 18,000ft odd, it's the highest mountain in Iran) and is varied with fearsome gorges, fantastically contorted rock strata, long curved rock tunnels, glissades of water slides, great spreads of avalanche debris and remote encampments of nomads. The variety of Persian landscapes, from salt-pan desert to rock gorge and precipice is further emphasised in the descent on the Caspian side, from tundra-type vegetation, through lush green forests - beach, oak, acacia, tamarisk and bracken - to a coastal plain of rice paddies, cotton and tobacco fields.

We then continued to Amol and Farah-Abad near the Caspian Sea to visit a sturgeon factory, where they produce caviar, and met some families on the beach there. Next stop was Mashhad, a place of religious pilgrimage, right up in the northeast corner of the country. I found it a fascinating city; the street that encircles the city precinct was lined with stalls and shops, as well as letter-writers, barbers, stilt-walkers, acrobats, beggars and the like, all plying their trade among the many folk on their pilgrimage to this holy city. In the heart of the city is the Holy Shrine of Imam Reza, which includes the 15th-century Goharshad Mosque.

From there, we headed towards Herat in Afghanistan and travelled through a sandstorm, which was quite scary. We couldn't drive more than 30 miles an hour, and we tried to catch up with a car in front of us so we could make sure we stayed on the road, but we soon couldn't even see the car. It was very frightening, but once we'd got through the sandstorm, we found ourselves on the wrong road – I think it was the 'donkey road' – but it was overlooking Herat below us. It was the most magical sight; Herat, with all of its twinkling lights, looked like the Arabian Nights all over again. Quite unforgettable.

We drove into Herat and, the next day, being a Friday, the streets were packed with people going about their work. We watched stonemasons making gravestones, men weaving cotton and silk goods on huge looms. There were fruit stalls, tea shops, carpet shops, people making shoes from worn-out rubber tyres, people selling thousands of buttons laid out on rugs. It was fascinating. We left Herat at dawn the next day, and what a great experience to see the red glow over the hills and the straight dark road ahead of us. The road was so straight you could actually see the Earth's curvature along the telephone posts lining the road. We were heading for Kandahar and we'd had to make sure we had enough fuel to complete the 200-mile journey without having to stop.

Around lunchtime, we stopped on the side of the road to refuel from our own petrol tank, and we saw a camel train preparing to load up. The kuchis (nomads) were sitting around a fire, cooking a mixture of ground maize and water that they'd pasted around a stone, and they offered us a taste of what looked to me like a shot put. It didn't taste much better either! The group sent a little boy to the local village to buy us some bread which, after considerable bartering, we paid a small fortune for.

We continued on our way to Kandahar, spent a night there and then travelled in a kind of 'U' up to Kabul, where we spent about three or four days. There we visited a zoo, and we used to walk up to hear the noonday gun, which I found really fascinating. It's part of the original fortifications of Sher Darwaza Hill and, every day at noon, it faithfully announces the noonday hour. Up on the hill, there was also a beautiful view of Kabul University and the snow-clad Paghman Mountains in the distance.

Well, we left Kabul, leaving behind the money racketeers near the bazaars (one pound on the black market was worth £2), cripples and beggars crying for money along the pavements, and men going to work relieving nature in the gutter. As we drove further out of the city, farmers were driving their stock to Kabul market; sheep, goats, camels, etc. lined the road as we began to feel the country air. Soon we had driven along the country plain and by the turn of a bend had entered the famous Kabul Gorge. From a wide fertile plain, the Kabul river toiled to enter the jaws and relentless throat of a cliff-gloomed cleft. The road squeezed past towering rock faces, with hairpins and tunnels, sometimes losing sight of the sky because of the overhanging rocks. We saw eagles hovering above as we stopped to take photographs. The gorge opened out onto the shores of a calm lake, turquoise blue against sheer brown slopes. Quite breathtaking, really.

Along the road, nomads (Kuchis) made a steady plod towards Jalalabad. Camels, donkeys, and children sat high, well-wrapped against the early breeze. Mile after mile the roadside was frequented by such trains. One or two camels even had donkeys placed in large sacks, sitting on top of them. At Jalalabad, we stopped at a petrol station to use up all our loose Afghan currency and then, within a short time, we had arrived at the Afghan-Pakistan frontier. Passports and permit checks were made and within the hour we were on our way towards the Khyber Pass into Pakistan.

The driving was now on the left, back to what we were used to it in England, and giving way to the people on the roundabouts. We had lunch, parked near the foot of the pass, where we were intrigued to see large old American cars carrying about 20 passengers, eight inside (four on each seat), five in the boot, five on the roof, and two on the bonnet, moving along at approximately fifteen miles per hour.

As passes go, the Khyber was invitingly mild. Its history and complexity of crags and savage hills give it the impressive fame that it truly deserves. We arrived at the summit; standing on a hill to one side of the road was a large fortress – 'Shagai Fort', home of the "Khyber Rifles". Signs along the mountain route gave one way for vehicles, and another for camels. Once over the Pass, fields became greener; trees lined the road; a hint of the good old British.

Our first stopover in Pakistan was in Peshawar, where we found that the locals loved English people. We had a lovely time there, made lots of friends, and were even allowed to go into the mosque, which was quite unusual. In the centre of the city there's an open bazaar, where the Street of Storytellers and the Street of Singing Birds were filled with brass and copperware merchants, shoemakers, dentists, potters, money-changers, people selling fruit, vegetables, peanuts and sweets. And, right next to all of the food, sanitation poured out from the houses all around. We didn't risk any lamb curries there...

The Indo-Pakistan war broke out in early December 1971, and we could feel the rumblings of war as soon as we arrived in Pakistan. There was a great deal of anti-India sentiment, as well as a lot of 'Kill India' and other war propaganda in the country at that time. It was quite unnerving, really.

After an hour's drive, we stopped near the road-crossing of the Indus. Here, the Attoch Fortress stands proud where the Kabul river joins the Indus; the British-built bridge is dual purpose - the rail runs about the road, only single-file with a garrison either end. There was no smoking, no cameras, although when we turned the bend, we managed to snap a quick shot. Rawalpindi soon appeared, centre of the Pakistan Army, but nothing more; the streets were similar to Peshawar, overcrowded and noisy. We left Rawalpindi for Lahore – a very pleasant drive.

The Badshari Mosque, built in the early 1670s, is one of the largest mosques in the world and architecturally unique, with its contrasting red sandstone pillars, towers and arches, and white marble domes. Nearby is the Maharaja Ranjit Singh's Samadhi, or shrine, of white marble, glaring in the sunlight almost like sugar. You could see the Pakistan Day Memorial from the arches of the Mosque, a tall tower of concrete with marble surrounds resembling the country's emblem – a five-pointed star and the new moon. We took a lift to the top, giving us a beautiful view over the city. and giving us a clearer view of the national emblem.

Amakali Bazaar was very interesting, with milling throngs and hundreds of tongas, weaving in and out of the traffic. This old part, near the city walls, was in a complete contrast to the large avenues, three-lane dual carriageways and modern buildings of the new part of town.

After spending the morning washing clothes by the canal, we drove to Hussienwale, the Pakistan-Indian frontier, relieved to find it still open.

We didn't visit anywhere else in Pakistan but after this kind of swoop through the country, we went on into India, where we immediately travelled north towards Amritsar. Things felt a bit tense there too because of the looming war, so we left after two nights, but not before visiting the 'mecca of the Sikhs', one of the holiest sites of Sikhism: the Golden Temple of Amritsar, which appears in stark contrast to its plain surroundings. It is absolutely stunning, and so quiet when you walk through it; you really get a sense of how sacred it is, even though, as a tourist, you can't stop and read the holy book or anything. You can't quite believe how special it is – the whole temple is gold, and exquisitely beautiful. When I went back to school and gave talks in assembly, I told the school about Amritsar and a young lad came up to me afterwards and told me he hoped to go and visit there, because he was a Sikh and knew all about the importance of that special temple.

From Amritsar, we drove along the winding Srinagar Pass. The road from Jammu to Srinagar in the vale of Kashmir can only be described as a continuous pass – hairpin bends for two-hundred mile, sweeping high into the mountains to a height of 11,570ft. Beautiful snow-capped ridges rise steeply on either side, eventually entering a fertile plain along which runs the river Jhelum. Here all the land is terraced. We stopped at Verriag to see the source of the river. Here the Mughals built a large garden and shrine, octagonal in shape, surrounding a pool from where the river Jhelum flows. Trout and other fish occupy the 50ft pool which flows through the gardens and along the plain to Srinagar.

Srinagar, the capital of Kashmir, is 5,200ft. above sea level. It is surrounded by mountains and is silvered with many lakes, the most celebrated being the Dal Lake. Srinagar is notable for its houseboats. These are floating, well-equipped houses with spacious upper decks, from which it is a joy to behold the sunset. Plying between the houseboats and the various lakes are the 'Shikaras', the Gondola of Kashmir. Srinagar is a fascinating city to explore. The bazaars display a profusion of wares – papier mache objects, silver and brassware, intricately carved woodwork in walnut and the beautiful woven carpets for which Kashmir is renowned.

We went to Gulmarg, which is reported to have the highest-altitude golf course in the world, at an elevation of 2,650 metres (8,690ft) above sea level, "The Meadow of Flowers". The view from there was breathtaking! Nanga Parbat – 26,000 ft. high – is one of the giants of the Himalayas, and spread below it, the whole Vale of Kashmir.

We took the same road (the only road) back down Srinagar Pass again, before setting off for our next stop – Delhi.

We stayed on the racecourse in Delhi, which is where we eventually managed to get rid of our stowaway mouse! It had travelled about 6,000 miles with us from Turkey, through Iran, Afghanistan, Pakistan and now into India, eating our food and, we thought, laughing at us from the safety of its unreachable hiding spot. Once we got to Delhi, we bought a humane mousetrap, put some cheese down and managed to catch the mouse and then let it go on the racecourse, with something of a ceremony; we never realised just how hard it was to outwit a mouse!

The racecourse was where all the taxi drivers stayed too. We'd sit and drink chai tea with them in the evenings, but one night we were told to put our lights out because there was a blackout. We were told it was a practice for war because it looked like the Pakistanis were going to invade. It was quite tense, really – we couldn't believe it.

Despite the threat of looming war, we made the most of our time in Delhi. We visited the superb, huge Red Fort (Lal Qila) – Delhi's most magnificent monument, and so-called because its walls are made of red sandstone. Conveying the strength and delicacy of the Moghul architectural taste, this historic fort in Old Delhi served as the residence of the Mughal Emperors in the 1600s. It's an irregular octagonal in plan, with two long sides on the east and west, and six smaller ones north and south. The circumference is about one-and-a-half miles. There are three gates – Lahore, Delhi and Elephant – the third being inside of Delhi Gate and guarded by two elephant statues.

We stayed on to watch the Son et Lumiere, a spectacular sound and light show that gave us an idea of the heritage of this UNESCO World Heritage Site.

New Delhi, or what I like to call English Delhi, was designed by the British architect Edwin Lutyens and inaugurated in 1931. It's just an area of the city, a huge open space where the parliamentary buildings are.

We drove south from Delhi to the famous Qulb Minar, a tower of victory started around 1200 AD, by the Muslim rulers of the slave dynasty. Near this tower is the famous Iran Pillar, made of pure malleable iron as early as the fourth century AD. The Muslims built the mosque next to the tower from 27 Hindu temples, giving it the temperature of both Islamic and Hindu architecture – the snake patterns alongside the calligraphy being good examples.

During the evening we took a walk up the road from the race course. The moon and stars made it very pleasant; clear sky and warm air.

Continuing further south-west to Jaipur, we passed the airport, as well as small villages, chaiolands, aultwaite open country on the fertile Jamuma plains. At Alwar, a policeman directed us on to the wrong road, taking us into rough rugged country; the road deteriorated, finally becoming just a rough stoned surface, winding in and out of small mountains. Eventually, we arrived at a fork in the road, where there was a chai stand. By the way, chai or tea is made by adding tea, milk and sugar, then beating it together and serving in cups or glasses. We asked for the way, only to discover that neither road existed on our map.

Jaipur, the capital of Rajasthan, reflects the many-sided splendour of the state, and is a fantasy set in terra cotta pink stone. The city is encircled by rugged hills, crowned with mediaeval fortresses, and a crenellated wall, broken by eight gates. Among the most famous buildings in this 300-year-old city is the Hawa Mahal, the Palace of Winds. This is a fantastical building with a honeycomb facade.

Maharajah Jan Singh designed the capital, after examining plans of European cities and studying Hindu treatises of architecture. Its gates! Its walls! Its palaces! Its houses, with latticed windows, with a colour which at sunset gleams like the heart of a rose! Pink is the blue of India!

From Jaipur we journeyed towards Agra, stopping for the night at Falehpur Sikri. Avenues of trees lined the road, fields of mustard cultivated for its oil formed a large band of yellow on either side of the road. This was the capital instead of Agra, ordained by Akbar. It took nine years to build a hard, weather-resisting sandstone. After being occupied for 17 years, it was deserted almost overnight for lack, it is said, of an adequate supply of water. As a result, after all the intervening years, it is not a ruin but a well-preserved palace within the seven miles of the city walls, completely empty again of Moghul architecture.

The Taj Mahal was built by Shah Jehan as a mausoleum for his Queen Mumtaz Mahal. It took 22 years to build. Its white marble reflecting the same rays is inlaid with jade, topaz, white marble lapis lazuli, cornetian jasper, onyx, and the like (pietro dura inlay). The Taj Mahal is everything people say it is - beautiful, romantic and peaceful, surrounded by gardens and fountains, plus three main archways.

In the evening, we parked near the Taj Mahal for a quick visit under moonlight. After we finished supper, there was a knock on the window and a policeman asked us to put out all lights, as India was under a State of Emergency, and Agra was under blackout. What a surprise! Nevertheless, at about 9pm we walked towards the Taj Mahal but, before we had entered, a typical Home Guard type of fellow shouted, "Keep to your positions!"

Unfortunately, no Taj under moonlight, so we returned to the van and went to bed, only to be awakened at 1.30am by a full alert siren and the clatter of guns. We got out of bed and looked outside; tracer flares were being fired, breaking out to a red glow just overhead. Something frightening, although exciting, with the Taj Mahal glowing white from the moon on one side and red from the flares on the other. Altogether, there were four alerts and four ALL CLEARS! It felt like we were in a war film, with all the ack-ack fire, lights flashing and noise all around us. We couldn't see anything, but it was just unreal, and really, really scary. We were glad to leave in the morning.

I mentioned that my mum had been worried about me, and it's not surprising, really, when I think about the moments like this, during our journey, when our lives flashed before our eyes. Looking back on it now, I realise how differently things could have ended. I'm pleased I'm still here to tell you about it. I actually think I may have nine lives.

We also saw Akbar's tomb at Sikandra. Here, in vast gardens of some 240 acres, monkeys, black buck, and other animals, roam freely.

Across the River Yamuma is one of the most exquisite examples of Moghal craftsmanship, the first experiment in white marble with pietro dura inlay – and hence a forerunner of the Taj – is the Itimad-ud-Daulah, tomb for Mumtaz Mahal's grandfather.

We drove 280 miles via Gwalior, arriving at Khajuraho, home of the 'incomparable' temple of Khajuraho, created by the Chandela Kings, a robust Hindu dynasty that held sway in North India from the ninth to the thirteenth century.

The temples are hung, as it were, with tapestries of stone carving and represent an art, probably unequalled anywhere in spirit and expression. Dedicated to Shiva, Vishnu and Brahma, the sculpture proudly affirms that the senses are in every way equal to the spirit, some erotic, others majestic.

Leaving the temple, we continued our journey to Benares, stopping for a night's rest at Satma. Along the roadside, we saw potters at their wheels, tailors sewing, and basket-makers busy at their craft.

Bodh Gaya in Bihar is to the Buddhists what Bethlehem is to the Christians and Mecca to the Muslims. The sacred place is situated in sylvan solitude, away from the din and bustle of town life, on the banks of the Niranjana River. It's probably the holiest of holy places associated with the life of Buddha and it was here that Sakyamuni attained supreme enlightenment and became the Buddha.

The temple, which is perhaps the oldest of its kind, has a large square platform, which rises in the form of a slender pyramid, becoming narrower until it reaches its cylindrical neck. To the west stands the world-renowned, sacred Peepal tree, known as the Bodhi tree, or the tree of enlightenment and wisdom. Surrounding the temple are several trees (Peepal) and scrubs, making it a pleasant as well as a religious place.

Outside the surrounding walls Tibetan monks and their families formed a large compound of tents, inside of which they were weaving rugs.

Back down in India, we moved on to Varanasi and Benaras on the Ganges River. The city has a central place in the Hindu traditions of pilgrimage, death, and mourning, where Hindus are carried down to the river to be burned on funeral pyres. The stench is unpleasant, people bathe and wash in the river too, but we found it totally bewildering.

We continued on on our way to Raxaul, breaking a wing mirror passing a cow cart! Raxaul is the town where all the tour buses park because they're too big to go over the pass into Kathmandu, and it's the place you start when you want to visit Mount Everest. You park there and take local buses along the very long pass and, when you get to the top, there's an observatory tower. Nine times out of 10 you can't see Mount Everest because of the mist, but on this occasion we managed to see it and I got a perfect photograph of it under blue, blue sky. That was quite exciting, really.

After we got back to Raxaul, we drove down into the Kathmandu Valley, where I saw step farming for the first time. They farmed rice on the terraced fields, and the women carried brushwood down for their fires. It was just lovely. We also visited the Swayambhunath Temple, which is full of monkeys (one of which snatched Don's sandwich out of his hand), and the Durbar Square in front of the old royal palace of the former Kathmandu Kingdom.

Having travelled through a number of different countries, cultures and habitations, through dirt squalor and poverty, colourful scenery and landscapes, deserts and plains, mountains and valleys, we had completed one main stage of our overland trip.

Our next stop was Calcutta, a city of huge contrasts between rich and poor, and where kids gathered around our van like ants. A guy came over and invited us to stay in the Cathedral of Calcutta, at a minimal cost per night, so that's what we did; it was like staying in a campsite, as we could use their toilets too. We were there for Christmas and our Christmas dinner in the Cathedral cost us one shilling and three pence each!

A Dr Ganguly came to the Cathedral to meet us and invited us back for a meal in his house and, of course, we jumped at the opportunity! Because Sandra wasn't Hindu, she was allowed to sit and eat with the men, but the Hindu women served the food and weren't allowed to eat until all of the men (and Sandra) had finished. It turned out that Dr Ganguly was the Editor of the All India Radio Calcutta and he invited us to talk on the radio about our travel experiences, which was quite a fun thing to do! Our brief moment of fame.

We visited a Jain Temple, several Indian Hindu temples, went up and down the river and across the Hogarth Bridge, and saw the beautiful, bright marble Victoria Memorial. This is the noblest monument in Calcutta, built of white marble, brought from Jodhpur Islands, burning fiercely against a brazen sky as a tribute to the Victorian Island's years of imperial greatness. It is said that the architects tried to make it a competitor to the Taj Mahal, with Moghul favour and vast gardens and lakes. Inside are many paintings and sketches of people and events during the time of British rule in India.

One thing I'll never forget about Calcutta was seeing their double-decker buses, similar to the London ones, with a flat plate that you jump on. The buses would have so many people on – and hanging out of it – that it was nearly touching the ground. And the trains were no different; there were often more people travelling on the roof than inside the train.

A few days after Christmas, we left Calcutta and set off for Madras to get our boat. We travelled past a huge, impressive Hindu temple called Konark, which is built on a carved chariot with 24 enormous horses and enormous wheels. We then stayed in Puri, a fishing village not far from there. Puri has been an important centre of pilgrimage for Hindus throughout the ages. The Jagannath Temple, built in 1198 AD by Ganga Deva, was dedicated to Sri Jagannath. of the Vaishnavite type. The height of the main structure is 65 metres. It houses three images – Sri Jagannath, his sister Subhadra, and elder brother Bulbhadra. There is a huge kitchen attached to the temple, which serves cooked food as offerings to the deities. The temple of Jagannath especially attracts crowds during the Rath Yatra (Car Festival – June and July), when the three Rathes – or chariots of Jagannath, Bulbhadra and Subhadra – are drawn through the streets of Puri.

It was fascinating to watch the village folk walk about half a mile to the fishermen as the boats went out. Each time the boat went out, they'd ceremonially break open a coconut on the bow, pouring the contents along the boat. They'd then give half of the coconut to the children, and the other half was a gift to the boat. They also cut the head off a chicken and ran their blood around the boat as the fishermen pushed it out, to make sure they'd bring in a substantial catch. A stream of people would greet the boat coming in, and the women would buy fish and take it back to the village in baskets or upturned turtle shells on their heads. It was just lovely.

This community spoke a different language from the people of Puri. They lived on the beach in palm-thatched huts, which they vacated during the summer months to return south to their homes, which are wonderful and lively, industrious, seen edging the Bay of Bengal.

Having spent three days on the beach, we left Puri for Chilka Lake, hemmed in between the green hills of the south and the sea in the north. It is India's largest freshwater lake, covering an area of 450 square miles, separated from the Bay of Bengal by a long sandy ridge. You could see grey and comb ducks, grey-leg car-headed geese, pintail, pochard, plovers, waders and, in rare cases, pink-headed ducks on the water. In addition, tiger, panther, boar, wild bears, bison, samba, spotted and barking deer, roam around in the surrounding forests and islands. In the nearby village of Rambha, we saw a man weaving sliced cane mats under the flickering light of his oil lamp.

We continued travelling south and got to Madras (Chennai) four or five days early, as we had to check the vehicle in for our boat trip to Penang. We stayed in the house Engelbert Humperdinck was born in, and we visited the markets, went to a festival, and took a train to Bangalore, which was an experience. We had to see about a dozen people before we even got our tickets, and then when we eventually got on the train, we found somebody else sitting in the seats we'd just been at pains to book!

We drove south of Madras to Mahabalipuram, famous for its seashore, temples and sculptures. It was a seaport built by an emperor of the Pallowa dynasty during the seventh century. One of the main attractions is the Arjuna's penance (Descent of the Ganges), which is a vast panel of relief sculptures depicting the mythical story of the river Ganges. The relief, measuring some 27 metres long and nine metres high, shows Arjuna in the act of doing penance. Two life-size elephants are among the numerous other animals, gods and angels.

Back in Madras, we went to get the van on the boat and I noticed Richard Packwood's name (a friend of our family back home) on the list, but they said he'd cancelled the booking. It turns out he'd just cancelled the booking for the vehicle, as he no longer had one, but he, his cousin and sister did still travel on the boat as foot passengers, so we spent our week on the boat together. The boat, called the Rajah, was the only steam-operated boat in the British colonies and we saw a plaque on the boat that said: '35 Europeans, 1,500 natives, only if the weather's fine.'

Our first stop was in Nagapatha, where we drove to the incredible, intricately carved Kapaleeswarar Temple. While we were there, there were boats bringing loads of onions onto the boat, and boats bringing the '1,500 natives' onto the boat. The natives all slept on the deck, in an area demarcated for them, which I felt very uncomfortable about – there were certain areas they could and couldn't go, and people could walk all around them while they were sleeping. There were bodies everywhere on the deck. And there was an incredible food production line going; each person who slept on the deck got two chapattis in the morning, and two in the evening, and the two guys making them never seemed to stop working! From there, we docked in George Town and made our way to beautiful Penang where, before the Packwoods left for Singapore, we all went to the snake temple and got some photos with snakes on our heads.

We drove the 300 miles from Penang to Bangkok, where someone had told us a good place to stay was the monastery. It was, and after the humdrum of our trip so far, it was really peaceful. We slept in our van and went out with the monks at half past five in the mornings, begging for rice and so on. We went to places that you wouldn't go to today, such as the Palace and the Stupas, and we rode on klongs along the river. Again, as with the Ganges River, I was bewildered to see people clean their teeth, wash their clothes and go to the toilet in the same water! We went to the Bridge over the River Kwai, and to the war cemetery linked to it, which was very fascinating and quite sobering.

We knew there was a very narrow strip of Burma (Myanmar), where there were terrorists and we'd been told they'd stop us and ask us for money. We'd been struggling to get our van into gear and it decided to break down on us in that exact strip of land, the most dangerous part of Thailand. There was a place in Penang that could repair it, but that was about 240 miles away, so Don and I decided to hitch the tow rope to the front and pretend to pull it along, with Sandra steering. A big, overloaded truck came along and, after a bit of haggling, the driver said if we gave him two quid, he'd tow us to the VW garage. We didn't know where that was, but we hitched up to him anyway. Going up some of the steep passes, the lorry would just stop, or go round and drag the van across the road – it was terrible, but we survived the 180km journey to a garage near the Malaysian border. And actually, this story has a happy ending: the mechanic took two days to fix the gearbox – the gasket between the gearbox and the clutch housing had perished, and the oil was coming through – and he charged us £9. It was £4.50 for taking out all the parts and putting them all back, and £4.50 for gaskets and oil. We'd expected a bill of £40, so that was a huge relief and a much better outcome than we feared!

We drove from there down to Himalaya and we went to the Cameron Highlands, a jungle area in the middle of Malaysia with lots of tea plantations. As we rounded a bend on a very nice, wide tarmac road, we came across a Sikwari tribesman with his wife and child crossing the road. We stopped and took a photograph of him, but he wanted something for it and we weren't going to argue as we'd seen he had poisonous arrows on him.

After calling in at a terribly British tea plantation, we went to a beach called the Blue Lagoon, where they happened to be filming a Dunlop advert. We watched for a bit and chatted with the crew and, because it was so hot, decided we'd sleep on the beach. We woke up crawling with insects!

It was there we also met an English-speaking Chinese gentleman who invited us back to his rubber plantation. His home was a huge mansion that had been built by a Scot, and it had four tennis courts on the vast grounds. When we arrived, memsaab took our bags inside but then the gentleman's wife had to come and perform a ceremony with rice to make sure the evil spirits didn't come in with us. Her husband then shouted to his servant to get the gun, and he promptly shot two or three squirrels, which we had for supper. We stayed there for two nights, and Don, who was an avid reader, loved spending time in their vast library.

From there, we continued onto Kuala Lumpur, where we needed to book the boat to Fremantle and arrange the transfer of funds from Lloyds Bank to the Binney Company.

That sorted, we drove into Singapore where we parked literally outside Raffles. We spent time with our friend, Richard Williams from Bristol, who we'd met on the boat. Richard told us he would be staying with his college friend, who was the son of the Chief of Police of Singapore, and invited us to join them in their beach house. We did, and the beach house was huge! They had a speedboat and we had a great time with them, waterskiing and all sorts. We were very lucky.

In Singapore, we also visited the bird park, which was fascinating; Sago Street, where religious families used to take their old to die; Wicoley Street, where people will cook whatever food you want; and we visited the gay area, where we weren't very welcome at all. We were just being nosy, really. Our week in Singapore was absolutely superb and we really enjoyed it.

We had to load our car onto the boat, the Cota Singapora, bound for Fremantle. We got dockside the day before departure so they could load the vehicle, but they told me I had to load it. They could lift only one of the hatches, so I had to put my vehicle in, nose down. It was just an absolute joke. We set off the next day on the boat, which was really just a kind of tank. Lots of people from Fremantle would come to Singapore and sail back again, so for them it was like a cheap, 12-day cruise. There was a swimming pool on board, but not much else to do, so when Don and I met two Dutch lads, the four of us got ourselves paid jobs on the boat, sorting out food in the freezer room. We worked 20 minutes out and 20 minutes in, and I always remember asking the chap if I could have a drink. He said yes, and gave us lager from Fremantle, as long as we didn't drink while we were working. So we gathered up the bottles every time he gave us some and stored them in the bath in our room. Every evening when we went for our meal, we'd have a bag of lager bottles under the table. We ended up with plenty of alcohol! And then, of course, I always remember crossing the equator and every bar was playing Waltzing Matilda.

When we got to Australia, the boat was impounded, and we couldn't get anything off it. We stayed with Don's brother in Perth, and I only managed to retrieve my van three days later. I wasn't really surprised to discover later on that the boat had been impounded because the hatches wouldn't open . . .

The van now had 18,500 miles on the clock and, about 180 days after leaving London, we'd reached our final destination. At this point of our journey, you may be interested in a few statistics:

Having been on the road for nearly 30 weeks:

- We'd completed 18,500 miles.
- We'd used 3,230 litres of petrol and six tyres.
- We'd consumed 700 eggs, 400 loaves of bread, 50 lbs of sugar, 40 lbs of potatoes, 35 lbs of rice, 25 lbs of spaghetti, 7 lbs of coffee, the contents of 400 tea bags, plus £25 worth of tinned food, 20 lbs of jam, and 12 packets of cornflakes.
- We'd used four airmail writing pads. sent 80 telegrams and 50 postcards.
- We'd used 25 rolls of toilet paper.
- Plus, I'd lost half the hair on my head but gained 12 lbs in weight.

And now this new continent, Australia, held new adventures for us.

Rebuilding the engine in the desert

Sandra in Shiraz (domes are a different shape). She had to cover her shoulders to enter the mosque.

Staff at the Roadside Police Station

*Persepolis - Looking out to Tent City before it was closed to the public for
2500 years of reign celebrations.*

Persepolis - The size of the sculptures! They are over 2500 years old.

The Caspian Sea

Mosque in Mashhad, Iran

Camel train in Southern Afghanistan travelling south to Quetta

Pump attendant, Afghanistan

The infamous Khyber Pass

Golden Temple Amritsar - Mecca for Sikhs

Red Fort Delhi

Vultures eating a dead carcass by the roadside.

The Tajmal Agra

Erotic sculptures covering the temples

Step farming in the Katmandu valley

Cathedral, Calcutta

Jain Temple Calcutta

Victoria Building, Calcutta

San Temple

The ornate carving at Konarka, The San Temple

Loading 1500 locals

Snake Temple Penang

Prisoners Cemetary near the bridge over River Kwai

Extracting latex from trees in Malaysia

Native family crossing the road in the Cameron Highlands

4. AUSTRALIA

After our short stay in Perth, Sandra got herself a job as a waitress in Ivy Springs, pretty much in the middle of nowhere, otherwise known as the Billabong. Don and I went to the Perth Labour Exchange and got jobs working on a farm 200 miles away, also in the middle of nowhere. Our instructions to get there went like this: drive to a town called Meridian, then 60 miles to another town called Mukinbudin then as far down the road as you can see for another 15-18 miles until you get to the bowser on the rail track, then turn right and it's the first house four miles in on the left. The directions actually worked, and when we got there, the farmer (Ray White, from Scotland originally) was working in the field, on the tractor. He stopped and came over to greet us and said he'd take us to our camp.

Our camp, our 'home' for the next while, was a really basic tin shed with two rooms, two beds and an outside toilet. This was a bit of a shock to the system for Don, who was a legal executive, and for me, a teacher, but we understood that most of the people who'd worked on the farm had been really rough, either drunks or of no fixed abode, so the accommodation wasn't pleasant at all. The shed had fly screens – an absolute necessity, we discovered – but they'd been slightly broken and the shed had been empty for about six months. I've never seen so many flies in my life. Ray gave us a huge can of fly spray, so Don and I masked ourselves and went in. Don sprayed and I followed and wiped the spray off, and then we went and sat in the van for about 15 minutes. I'm not joking when I say that when we went back in we were shovelling the flies out of that shed. It was really horrible, but then having done that massive purge, it was never that bad again.

Ray told us there were two aboriginal men who were also working on the farm, but we only saw them after three days. It was quite sad, really, because they'd work for a day and then take their $10 pay, buy wine with it and sit on the railroad track, drinking. Until they needed the next $10, and then they'd repeat the cycle. Ray would often ask us if we'd seen them, and I felt bad to have to say I hadn't; it felt like I was tattling on them.

Don and I started work straight away. It was tough, physical work. Our job was to pick roots (mallees) to clear the land for sowing with corn. We'd pick the roots and pile them in a pyramid so Ray could burn them in the evening. We'd end up literally black with roots, but often also black with flies. We wore hats with corks on them to stop the flies from getting into our eyes, but then when we sweated, our backs would end up black with flies. We kept a massive can of fly spray with us and we'd just constantly spray our backs.

After we'd worked for a week, Ray told us he needed one of us to drive the tractor, and asked which one of us would do it. I said it would be better if he decided which one of us, and he chose me. And then, after a fortnight, when he told us he couldn't keep us both on, he said one of us had to go, and again he asked us which one. Again, I asked him to make that decision, but then Don volunteered to go. Ray said he would have chosen me to stay anyway. So I drove Don back down to Perth, stayed the night there and drove back on the Sunday – that was quite a lonely drive, really, because not only was I on my own for the first time in months, I also had to go back into the bush to work on my own. But I was grateful I had a job and I really needed the money, so I just got on with it.

Ray expected everyone who worked for him to work hard. I knew what it was like to work on a farm, having grown up on one, so whenever he told me where and when he needed me to go, no matter what time of night or day it was, I'd make sure I was there half an hour before. He soon got me working a 16-hour shift, from midnight to four o'clock in the afternoon. I'd drive my van up to the tractor, get on the tractor and start working, and the guy who'd come off the tractor would drive my van to where his car was parked and then he'd drive home. When he took over from me at four o'clock again, he'd drive me to my van and I'd go home. It worked well.

Ray made a big impression on me because of how hard he worked. He'd just work, work, work. I was working because I wanted the money, but he was working because he didn't know any different. Some things he did were just crazy in my book, for example driving 75 miles just to get some bits and parts for the machines so he could come back and repair them himself.

Ray and his wife had two sons and, because of my teaching background, I soon started helping them with their homework. They weren't much interested in schoolwork as they just wanted to be on the farm, so their mum was really pleased that I was encouraging them and helping them with their work. Plus, that earned me a meal with the family in the evenings! We'd often catch a sheep, slit its throat, skin it and then cut it all up, and that was our meal – a real feast!

Life was quite lonely on the farm. Often the family would go out to the club or whatever, and I'd often volunteer to take the boys to the drive-in or to do something to keep them (and me) from getting bored! Sometimes I'd go to the bar and play pool, and once, after I won against a guy who was pretty useless, a couple of aboriginal men started to bet on me and they actually made some money! I'd also sometimes play badminton, and one guy I played against used to do a 150-mile round trip to play badminton. Life was quite different and distances were quite something in the middle of the Australian bush!

Once, in the middle of a friendly badminton match, someone came in and shouted that there was a fire in the railway station. Two of the lads were firemen. They ran to their truck while I took the others in my van. We got there first, as the fire truck wouldn't start, but we saw the burning train wagon with all of its canvas burnt off the main wood frame. When the fire service eventually arrived, they discovered no one had filled the water tender from the last time, so the best thing they could do was unhitch the wagon and push it down the road to burn itself out!

I had a few close shaves too, working on the farm. One night, I was woken up feeling really strange. It felt like something had bitten me and my skin began to itch, but when

84

I also started to sweat, things escalated quickly. I had a fever and I didn't really know where I was. I knew I had to be at the tractor at midnight, so I jumped in my van and, even though I couldn't see properly, I managed to get to the tractor. I told the guy I was feeling rough and needed to go home. He asked me if I'd used the outside toilet, and I said I had, and he said I must have been stung by a redback, a tiny little spider that runs around under the seat of the toilet and whose poisonous bites can be fatal. I asked if he thought I should go to hospital, but the guy said if I'd survived so far, I must have got through the worst. I went home and slept for a few hours and then went back to work, feeling a lit bit more normal. At the end of that day I went back into the toilet and saw the redbacks running all the way around the seat, so I threw kerosene on the toilet and set it alight. After that I decided I'd go in the bush rather than risk another bite from one of those little blighters. I could easily have died right there in that shed.

In another incident in which I could have died, it was raining and Ray told me to help him in the barn. In Australia, they'd often take the front axles off the tractor, and then hitch it to another tractor to make what's known as a tandem tractor. Ray wanted to take the axle with all the wheels on it, put it into the ute, and then drive it 50 miles to a farmer who wanted it. So in this big barn, there's a beam up top and he'd strapped a block and tackle to it, on a big hook. The plan was to lift the machinery up on the block and tackle, put the ute underneath it and then put the tractor in it. As the weight grew heavier, the whole block and tackle suddenly came down, touching my nose en route to the ground, where it made a massive hole. Ray decided to call it a day; we both knew I could have been killed instantly. That was another very close call.

After I'd worked for Ray for three months (February, March and April), I felt it was time for me to move on, so I went to tell Ray I'd be finishing at the end of April. He'd agreed to pay me $1.25 an hour and, although I'd always been willing to do everything he told me and he knew he could count on me, I was always careful to keep a note of how many days and how many hours a day I'd worked. During those three months, I'd managed to live for next to nothing – I had free accommodation, I got many free meals, and although I didn't travel much, I got free petrol (Ray had his own petrol tank on the farm). As a way of saving as much as I could, I'd asked Ray to pay me one lump sum at the end of the three months.

On my last day of work, he came to see me and invited me over for a meal and, although there was a lot of drinking that evening, I kept myself reasonably sober. I got home at three o'clock in the morning and then got woken up at the crack of dawn with the sound of a tractor – it was Ray, already hard at work. When I went to tell him I was all packed and ready to go, he told me to go and have a coffee in the garden. A very old friend of Ray's was there too and, when Ray asked me how much he owed me, I told him I'd worked a thousand-and-something hours and he owed me nearly $2,000. His friend couldn't believe it. Ray said, 'Taff's the only worker who's ever come to work for me that I've never ever had to call to wake up to come to work.' And with that he wrote out that cheque and gave it to me, thank you very much.

I drove back to Perth, where I met up with Don and Ann (Richard Packwood's sister) and the three of us started our Australian road trip. We drove to Margaret River in Western Australia, to Albany and then around to Norseman.

Margaret River is a picturesque town, 200 miles from Perth. It is most attractively situated on its river between timbered slopes of karri, jarrah and redgums. Further south is Augusta, made important by the opening of a new cave in 1958. This cave is one of the largest underground cavities in Western Australia - one of the most fascinating features that meets the eye on entry is the Grand Straw that measures 19' 4 ½" - the longest-recorded straw of its type in the world. Other features are the karri forests and organ pipes, which reflect their beauty in the still clear water of the lake.

Cape Leeuwin is the extreme south-west point of the continent, where the Indian and Southern oceans meet. It was from the Dutch ship 'Leeuwin' that this part of the state was first seen in 1622, hence its name. The lighthouse on the top of the peninsula guides and guards shipping along the treacherous coastline.

Although it was mid-winter (July), it was a pleasant drive through the karri forests near Pemberton, where we stayed a night near a 300 -ft-tall karri tree with a lookout point on the top. They used this spot to check the wind direction and speeds, and it also served as a fire lookout.

After spending a few days on a settlement farm near Albany, we continued our journey to Esperance and northward to Norseman. The flat countryside of scrub-like vegetation - a complete contrast to the forests of karri -

stretched for miles, with small hillocks breaking the horizon. Dull winter weather gave it a cool barren look and the odd farm sign, windmill and house broke the monotony of what was otherwise constant scrubland.

Norseman was our turning point east to face the vastness of the Nullarbor Plain. Fortunately, the road to the West Australian border was a bitumen road, making the boring drive at least comfortable. As the trees thinned, a flat brown plane emerged, leaving me with the remainder of the farm at Mukin Cudin.

At one stage the road was straight for 90 miles, just an undulating strip of tarmac. When darkness fell, driving became hazardous as kangaroos, attracted by the vehicle lights, sat on the road, at times only to be moved by my bumper. You could see the sea from Eucla, a resting point before we began the long 300-mile trek of untarmacked road, losing an hour and a half of time.

As we crossed into South Australia, we left a trail of dust, blinding any vehicle following within a mile or so. It took us nearly 40 miles to pass the huge trucks, travelling some one or two miles slower. We had to wait until the wind was in the right direction. It was quite scary.

We were pleased to reach our halfway point at Ivy Tanks, where we filled up with fuel and water. Petrol was 30 percent more expensive here than in Perth. Water was taken from boreholes or rainwater from huge tanks situated under a covering of zinc sheets. Driving along the Nullarbor was so different, every vehicle you met waved frantically with excitement at the side of a motor car. All along the roadside, burned-out cars scarred the countryside – a stark reminder that not everyone makes it to Ceduna or Eucla.

The biggest magnet for winter visitors is the Kosciusko Snowfalls. Most of the million-and-a-quarter-acre Kosciusko National Park, which stretches from Canberra to the Victoria border, is covered with snow during winter and spring. Lake Eucumbeni, the largest of the man-made lakes, is also a centre for tourists, with facilities for camping, fishing, and so on.

Beautifully coloured birds added to the pleasant scenery – a reminder of home – and the road took us on to Canberra.

Canberra's history is fairly short, beginning in 1909 after the Federation of the Australian States. The area was virtually uninhabited, but when we were there, 136,000 people lived in this Garden City, and there were six million trees in the national capital.

The main attractions had certainly been produced to impress the tourists, such as the Carella and water jet, which can be seen from nearly any part of the city. One notable factor - Canberra has no pavements. The apparent reason, I guess – wealth!

Some 25 miles from the city, in a nature reserve, is a relaxing forested area set aside to preserve animal life in its own environment. Emus, kangaroos, koalas, rosellas, kookaburras and the like run freely. Nearby, the Americans have built a tracking station for the Moon programme. At present, they are tracking a satellite on the way to Jupiter. It should pass close to the planet this November. But they have to continue to keep in contact with it for the next five years - travelling at the same speed.

From the Nullarbor Plain, we travelled right up to Cape York and back down to Adelaide, where our road trip ended and the three of us went our separate ways. I travelled to Sydney to stay with John Kay, my friend that I'd gone to Australia to see, and to start thinking about my journey home. It was the end of another key stage of our trip.

Farming in the bush, Western Australia

Flying over the Atolls in the Pacific

Termite mound

Vast empty beaches in Queensland

5. THE WAY BACK

John and his wife were both teachers and when I said I needed to earn some money to get home, they suggested I call up a few schools to see who needed a teacher. So that's how I ended up having a really great six weeks, teaching manual arts at a fantastic school called Pittwater High School in Sydney. Manual arts included technical drawing, woodwork and metalwork, and I found it a little bit different from the technical subjects I taught in Bristol, where we'd moved on and were doing plastics and hand casting and everything. At Pittwater, I was teaching more woodwork and it was all a lot more hands-on, but I loved it.

The school was a very wealthy school. It had a tuck shop, where you could buy anything you wanted or needed, whether it was a pen, a pencil, food, tuck, drinks, books, whatever. I learnt that they were turning over about $10,000 a month, which I thought was phenomenal; a real business!

I also got involved in the Wednesday afternoon sports, taking the youngsters out sailing. I knew nothing about sailing, but because the school attracted children from wealthy families, most of the pupils in the sailing club had their own boats, or their families had their own boats, so they got me involved and on board. I couldn't believe I was getting paid to spend Wednesday afternoons sailing in Sydney – it was just absolutely lovely. One of the youngsters ended up crewing on the Australian boat that won the America's Cup, so that was quite something.

When my six weeks were up, it was time for me to go home. I also knew I had to sell my van, which had by then clocked up about 28,000km after faithfully carrying us all the way from London to Australia, and then all around Australia. I've often thought about that van and wondered if it's still on the road. It was a split-screen VW Kombi, which would certainly be worth something today. With the proceeds of the sale, I splashed out US$90 on an open ticket that could take me anywhere, as long as it was in the direction of London and left for home.

My first leg of hedge-hopping took me from Sydney to Noumea in the Caledonian Islands, on to the New Hebrides, Tanna Island and Fiji.

Vila, head of the administration for the New Hebrides, is on the island of Ejate. A trip around the island takes some four hours, about 75 miles. The road deteriorates from a bitumen surface near Vila, to sand and gravel and mainly coral, to a grass track in the northern part. The beautiful blue sea was so enchanting as one drove in and out of the vast coconut plantation - now left to rot due to the expense of labour to extract the copra.

Pawpaw and mango trees hanging with fruit were ready for the taking. A large magnesium mine at Farrie in the centre employed only a handful of natives, while a ghost train showed what prosperity once lay within this mine.

Oak-rigged canoes still ferried people between the islands. At one village we visited on our journey around the island, the natives were weaving mats from thin strips of wood. Some were for sale, others were used as gifts during a marriage celebration.

I was fortunate enough to get a free ride on a trading vessel to Tanna Island, 140 miles southeast. We left Vila at dusk and by 3.30am, we were well out to sea. Waves were covering the deck and bridge. I had already lost my last three meals. The bows dipped heavily into the sea, rocking the 50ft boat so much that I could not get to sleep.

I was asked if I could steer a boat and I said I could if I had a compass. Anyway, there I was steering this small boat in the dark, and then somebody said those words you never want to hear on a boat: 'Man overboard!' There was a bit of a scramble, and I then discovered there were 17 Tannese people travelling on the boat with the cargo.

We dropped anchor 24 hours later at Lenakel Bay, a picturesque setting but a treacherous reef surrounding it. The Paul family met us with a jeep and took us home. We had something to eat and then I was relieved to be able to go to sleep. When I woke up, I noticed my clothes had all been washed and were hanging on the clothes line outside. It was quite the luxury, after all the months of travelling and living so frugally. It was very, very nice.

Tanna is one of the few islands that still has mystic traditions: the John Frum Cargo Cult. On the arrival of an American GI with vast quantities of equipment during World War II, it made such an impression on the local leaders that they kept in touch by radio (a crude resemblance of radio and aerial), hoping that one day John Frum would return, bringing them everything desired by man – Tanna.

A fortnight previously, a light aircraft had crashed on the "white grass" killing one passenger. So the excitement of chasing the "wild horse" in a Land Rover across the large "white grass" was slightly dulled, knowing that in two or three days I would be travelling back to Ejab using the same type of aircraft.

On my last night with the Paul family, we left for a trip across the island to visit the volcano. For the 15 or so miles to the base of the volcano, we talked about how fantastic and frightening it was, and how at times people had been injured with rocks blown from inside the crater.

It took us half an hour to climb the rather steep ascent of 900ft. The noise was incredible and the thunder and red glow in the sky was really frightening. A 50-yard walk along its flat top brought us to the edge of the crater, from where you looked down some 900ft to the red glowing boreholes below and, as the noise and vibrations collect the eruptions, it throws out red hot lava some 800ft into the air, leaving the crater a massive red glow. Small boreholes continually hissed and grunted, throwing up ash and dust.

We stood for an hour. I was just mesmerised, watching and waiting for the large holes to erupt. Unfortunately, we had to leave, but the noise and heat underfoot kept reminding me how active the volcano was.

The boys, who were constantly taking tourists to this volcano, said that it was working hard that evening, but on some nights, they had seen it throwing up lava over the top.

And no-one could get near enough to climb it. As we left along the edge of the lake beneath, we could see that on occasion red hot lava appeared on the skyline.

When I got to Fiji, I got chatting to an American girl on the bus, who worked for the peace corps. She invited me to the village where she was living, so I went with her and, of course, if you're a foreigner visiting one of these villages, you have to have a ceremony with the chief. I think it's just an opportunity for you, as the visitor, to buy them kava and for them to drink it! I stayed there for a few days and ended up being invited to a local wedding too. It was the first time I'd ever seen food being cooked in the ground: they put the food in the ground, made a fire around it, covered it with stones and then added a top layer of leaves. Three days later they opened it up and the meat was cooked. It was delicious.

After leaving the village, I visited a gold mine near Mount Victoria and experienced another first. I got talking to the mine manager and, as it happened, he was a Welshman who'd been mining in South Wales. He offered to take me down the mine, which I'd never done before, and it was really very interesting. I still have a rock with gold specks in it that he gave me; I've kept it all these years.

From there I flew to Tonga and then on to Western Samoa, and into the main town called Apia. The first thing I saw was a policeman wearing a skirt, directing traffic. I thought he'd be a good person to ask where the best place was to stay, so I went up to him and asked. He said I could stay at the police station and sleep on the balcony, so that's what I did. The next day, I left my stuff there to go and explore the island. I had an idea of where I wanted to go, and the island wasn't very big anyway, so I hitch-hiked my way around. At about midday, a chauffeur-driven car pulled up, and the mother and her 18-year-old daughter in the back offered me a lift. I asked where they were going and they said they didn't know, what did I suggest? So I told them I was going to a waterfall and told them a bit about it, so they thought that sounded like a good idea. They said they'd give me a lift, so they invited me into the car and said I could sit next to the driver. I ended up being their tour guide, which was quite fun! The next day, the daughter and I went to see Robert Louis Stevenson's grave, and her mum was so pleased she invited me to join them for a meal in the hotel that night.

In the meantime, when I'd gone back to the police station, my police officer friend told me I had to go to the immigration office as they weren't at all happy about my sleeping there. I went and met with the immigration officer, a very surly German guy who was really unreasonable. He asked me all sorts of ridiculous questions, including why I was staying in the police station and not in a hotel, and he gave me a really hard time. He wouldn't listen to anything I had to say, and just kept telling me I shouldn't be on the island at all. When he stood up and said I'd have to leave, I literally slammed my fist on his desk and told him I had my visa and that meant I was entitled to stay on the island. He glared at me but didn't say anything. When I walked out of his office, all the typists and staff in the office must have been listening, and they cheered. Back at the police station, my friend said he'd spoken to his dad and he was happy for me to go and stay with them, in a hut at the bottom of the family's garden. They'd all heard about the stir I'd caused at the immigration office! Turns out he was the most hated man on the island. 'Everybody's happy in Western Samoa, and he's the only person no one likes. He just doesn't fit in.' That made me feel a bit better.

I then learnt that my police officer friend's father was the Private Secretary to the Prime Minister of the island. He'd just recently been to Manchester, where he and his Prime Minister had met with Ted Heath, the then British Prime Minister.

When I went off to the hotel to have a meal with the lady and her daughter, they told me they'd met someone at the hotel and had invited him to join us at the table. It turns out he was from Welshpool in Wales, which is where my brother lived. We were in the middle of the Pacific and discovered this coincidence, it was absolutely incredible!

From there, I went to Tahiti, where I met a Scottish family who'd been sailing around the world on a catamaran. The parents lived on one side of the vessel, their two children on the other, and in the middle was the school where the children had to do three hours of schoolwork every day. It was St Andrew's Day when I met them, and they invited me on board to join them in their celebrations.

After Tahiti, I flew to Acapulco in Mexico, where I saw the Elvis Presley dive, onto Mexico City, where I went to the Guadeloupe Festival, and then on to Bermuda, my final stop. When I got to the airport to fly back to London, they asked me if I'd paid for my ticket. They wanted money but I had none, so they eventually let me onto the plane. I was almost stopped at the final hurdle, but I got back to London and my brother met me at the airport. December 1972, 16 months after I'd left London with Don and Sandra, I'd got to the end of the trail.

I was excited to see my mum, as I think she'd worried about me quite a lot, especially when she saw things on the news, like the Indo-Pakistan war and so on. But funnily enough, I think my dad was more thrilled about my trip than my mum was, even though he'd been so unsupportive of my going in the first place. He had discovered everybody had been following me through the newspapers and he seemed to like hearing people say they'd just been reading about his son. Underneath it all, I do think he was proud of me.

Natives of Tanna Island

Bibi cyclone 1972

Flying Fox, Tonga Island

Fishing in Samoa

Sun and Moon Temples outside Mexico City

Mexico City

6. JUST A LAD FROM LLANDINAM

I wanted to write this book so my grandchildren might realise Grandpa isn't perhaps the boring old bugger they thought he was! It was quite something back then to take on a trip all the way from London to Australia by road, whereas now, everybody travels because it's easy to do. Communication is so much easier today too – at the touch of a button, you can be in touch with anyone anywhere in the world. In the 1970s, I'd have to go to the post office every time I wanted to send a letter, which could then take two or three weeks to reach its destination. No wonder my poor mum worried so much.

I learnt a lot about tolerance on the trip too, especially through meeting different people and experiencing cultures that were new to me and, I guess, through living in such close quarters with Don and Sandra in the van. The trip also opened my eyes to things I'd never known at home, such as the extreme poverty in Calcutta, where parents would break their children's arms and legs so they could get more money when begging, and people dying from cold on the streets of Kabul.

Looking back on the whole experience now, one thing I'd have done differently was I'd have become an Australian citizen. The school wanted me to do that so they could offer me a permanent job, but I just wanted to travel through the Pacific and get back home. I guess if I hadn't, I wouldn't have met and married my wife, so there's that. But it's something I've thought about a lot; having Australian citizenship would have made a lot of things easier for me.

I also wanted this book to give my friends and family a basic understanding of why I went on the trip. When I got back to school, I went into the staff room and it struck me quite profoundly that nothing had changed. The same people sat in the same seats, playing the same bridge. It was the same group, except for me, and they were doing everything the same. Having had all of the experiences I'd had over the past 16 months, where I'd learnt so much about different people, different ways of life, and had my eyes opened to so many different ways of life, this felt very 'stuck' to me.

One of my teacher friends said to me, 'Meurig, the problem is, we couldn't do that. I couldn't do that.' My response was that anyone could do it if they set their mind to it. There was nothing magical that came out of the air to make me any different from anyone else and do things differently from anyone else. I'm just an ordinary lad from Llandinam, nothing special, who dreamt of faraway places and of travelling the world. And what happened was, I did it.

MY JOURNEY

1st September 1971, I left London for Dover ...

UK
London
Dover

Belgium
Ostend
Through **Belgium** to **Germany** and on to the **Austrian** Alps
Salzburg
Graz

Yugoslavia
Varaydin
Zagreb
Belgrade

Greece
Titov Veles
Thessaloniki
Kavala
Alexandroupolis

Turkey
Istanbul
(by ferry to) Üsküdar
Izmir-Bursa
Çanakkale
Izmir

Ephesus and Ruins of Troy
Aydin
Denizli to see Pammakali
Antalya
Konya
Ankara
Silifke
Sivas
Ezrincan and Ezurum
Mount Ararat

Turkey/Iran border – Bazargan
Maku
Marand
Tabriz
Mianeh
Zanjan
Qazin
Tehran
Qom
Isfahan
Persepolis
Shiraz
Abadeh
Shadeh

Tehran – 7,000 miles
Amol near the Caspian Sea
Sari

Farah-Abad on the Caspian Sea
Gorgan
Bojnurd
Quchan
Mashhad – 8,000 miles
Taybad

Afghanistan
Herat
Kandahar
Kabul
Jalalabad

Pakistan
Peshawar
Rawalpindi
Lahore
Kasur
Husseinwala (the border)

India
Ludhiana
Pathankot
Jammu – 10,000 miles
Srinagar
Amritsar
Kammu
Pathankot
Amritsar

Delhi
Jaipur
Fakhpur Sikri
Agra
Gwalior
Khajuraho
Satna
Benares
Sarnath
Patna
Muzaffarabad

Nepal – 12,500 miles
Raxaul
Kathmandu

India
Biranji
Motihan
Muzaffarpur
Bihar
Calcutta (Kolkata)
Kharagpur
Bhubaneswar
Konakara – 14,000 miles
Puri
Chilika Lake
Gopalpur
Visakhapatnam

Vijayawada
Madras (Chennai)
(trip to Bangalore – south Mamallapuram shore temples)

Malaysia
Penang (by boat)
George Town
Butterworth

Thailand
Hat Yai
Takua Pa
Ranong
Churn-Phon – 16,000 miles
Hua Hin
Bangkok (Kanchanaburi Death Railway)
Pathom
Chumphon
Ranong – 17,000 miles
Hat Yai
Sadoo

Malaysia
Ipoh
Kuala Lumpur – 18,000 miles
Malacca

Singapore – 18,500 miles

Australia
Fremantle (by boat)
Perth
Kalgoorlie
Perth
Margaret River
Karri (near Pemberton)
Albany
Esperance
Norseman
Nullarbor Plain
Yulara
Ceduna
Port Augusta
Adelaide
Coombe
Melbourne
Canberra
Sydney
Cairns
Mossman National Park
Sydney (sold van with about 28,000 miles on the clock)

Nouméa (New Caledonia)
New Hebridean Islands
Port Vila
Tanna Island, Vanuatu
Fiji
Tonga

Western Samoa
(American) Samoa
Tahiti

Mexico
Acapulco
Mexico City
Bermuda via Tampa Florida

UK
London

Date.	Country	Stop.	Miles Heading.	Petrol	Cost	Miles
31·8·71	Britain	Bristol	75316	√ FULL	£2·12·	
31·8·71	"	London.	75506	√ 15 gallons	£5·02½	75566
1·9·71	Belgium	Ostend	75586	√ 22·0 litres	205 franc	75670
2·9·71	Germany	Frank-furt.	75978	√ 30·00 litres	18·90 D/M	75861
				34·50 "	21·90 D/M	76081
3·9·71	Austria	Salzburg	76366	√ 19·50·	66·20 sch.	76357
4·9·71	Yugoslavia	South Zagreb	76700	√ 33·0 "	59·6 dinar	76500
				31·70	57·0 dinar	76711
5·9·71	Greece	border.	77236.	27·00 "	49·0 dinar	76898
				(2 gallons in) 14·50 "	4 gallons in 100 Drac	77244
6·9·71	Kavala"	Kavala.	77450.	15·3 "	94 Drac.	77390
7·9·71	Turkey	Istanbul	77703	30·4 "	48·00 TL	77539
				50·00 "	76·00 TL	77711
11·9·71	"	Canakale	78039	36·00 "	57·00 TL	77930
12·9·71	"	Izmu.	78241	Super. 34·80 "	72·45 TL	78119
13·9·71	"	Denizli	78486	35·20 "	55·00 TL	78336
14·9·71	"	Antalya	78666	31·90 "	51·00 TL	78525
15·9·71	"	Anamur	78874	36·50 "	57·00 TL	78735
16·9·71	"	Konya	79140	28·60 "	44·00 TL	78899
				32·70 "	51·00 TL	79054
17·9·71	"	Ankara	79268	30·70 "	50·00 TL	79229
18·9·71	"	Ankara-Sivas	79365	31·20 √	50·00 TL	79335
19·9·71	"	Sivas	79629	30·3 "	50·00 TL	79538
				31·6 "	54·00 TL	79691
20·9·71	"	Erzincan-Erzurum	79815	18·2 "	30·00 TL	78811
21·9·71	"	Agri.	80041	22·8 "	38·00 TL	79915
				17·0 "	28·80 TL	80098
22·9·71	Iran	Merand.	80266	24·0 "	144 Rs.	80146

Total £24

Total £12·25 TL
£22·30.

StoryTerrace

Milton Keynes UK
Ingram Content Group UK Ltd.
UKHW021131171123
432740UK00010B/155